BRICK OF

DAD HACKS

Brick of Dad Hacks:
Tips, Tricks, Shortcuts and
Dad-isms for Easy Parenting

13-Digit ISBN: 978-1-64643-267-7
10-Digit ISBN: 1-64643-267-3

This book may be ordered by mail from the publisher. Please include $5.99 for postage and handling. Please support your local bookseller first!

Books published by Cider Mill Press Book Publishers are available at special discounts for bulk purchases in the United States by corporations, institutions, and other organizations. For more information, please contact the publisher.

Cider Mill Press Book Publishers
"Where good books are ready for press"
PO Box 454
12 Spring Street
Kennebunkport, Maine 04046

Visit us online! cidermillpress.com

Typography: Clarendon, Hanley, Helvetica, Industry Inc., Sofia Pro

Printed in China

1 2 3 4 5 6 7 8 9 0
First Edition

BRICK OF

DAD HACKS

TIPS, TRICKS, SHORTCUTS AND DAD-ISMS FOR EASY PARENTING

CIDER MILL PRESS

BOOK PUBLISHERS
KENNEBUNKPORT, MAINE

CONTENTS

INTRODUCTION
6

CHAPTER 1:
DISTRACT HACKS
9

CHAPTER 2:
KEEP IT CLEAN
HACKS
27

CHAPTER 3:
OUT & ABOUT
HACKS
73

CHAPTER 4:
SAFETY HACKS
111

CHAPTER 5:
SNACK HACKS
147

CHAPTER 6:
FUN AT HOME
HACKS
167

CHAPTER 7:
MISCELLANEOUS
DAD HACKS
189

INTRODUCTION

So, you're a dad? Congratulations! Maybe you're new to the role, or maybe you've had some experience. In either case, you probably already know that you need all the help you can get. Being a dad these days is different than it was even a few decades ago. Long gone are the days when the man would leave the house, go to work for the day, and the wife would stay home and look after the kids. The "Leave it to Beaver" model for families and parenting has changed pretty drastically, and honestly, men are better for it.

Dads these days might be stay-at-home caretakers for their kids, or they and their spouse might both work. Maybe they're lucky enough to work from home, especially in the wake of the pandemic. Regardless of their situations, most dads want to be involved in their children's lives, from infancy all the way through the dreaded teenage years. They want to change diapers, burp their babies, play with their daughters and sons, make sure they eat properly, and do all the things that parents do. Those things have often been labeled "moms' work" in the past. But dads can take part in all those activities too, and find them to be fun and rewarding.

If you enjoy "dadding" but sometimes feel like you could use a little bit of extra help, this book is for you! It won't give you advice on parenting how-tos or any of the difficult stuff, but for dads with children between their infancy and teen years, some of these hacks might be just the thing you need to make your life a little easier.

This book offers 100 tips, tricks, and simple hacks that can be helpful to you in a multitude of situations. Feel free to dip in and try a new one every day! If you have a baby, you'll have a full selection of 100 ideas you can use as your child grows. If your kids are already a bit older, you won't need some of the tricks for babies and toddlers (though you might wish you'd had them back then). But you'll still have numerous hacks that can make their days more enjoyable and yours a little easier.

Nothing suggested here takes a lot of work to set up or is overly complicated; that's the whole point of hacks. These tips are "why didn't I think of that" ideas that will smooth things along and give you some real help with minimal fuss or effort. You might already know about some of these ideas—there are a lot of parenting websites out there that offer ideas for hacks of all kinds, and you may have browsed some of them. But this way, you have a good selection of tips in one handy little book that you can refer to again and again.

Being a dad is an adventure like no other. It's a wonderful journey you take with your spouse or on your own, and is one of the most rewarding things you can do. Explore a great selection of ways to make parenting even more enjoyable with the *Brick of Dad Hacks*!

CHAPTER 1

DISTRACT HACKS

HACK #1:

IF THEY'RE OLD ENOUGH, HAVE YOUR KIDS WASH YOUR CAR WHILE YOU WORK.

Is it a hot (or even warm) day? Do you have things to do outside and need to keep your kids busy for a bit? Have them put on clothes that are okay to get wet, and hand them a couple of buckets of soapy water and some sponges. Ask them to wash your car. It doesn't matter if they do a great job (you can always rinse it off with a hose later). The fun of splashing water and soap around will keep them busy for quite a while, and the bonus is: you get a clean(ish) car.

HACK #2:

DOES YOUR KID HATE BATH TIME?

TOSS SOME GLOW STICKS IN THE BATHTUB.

Snap a few glow sticks and let them sit in the water. Turn off the lights. Bring in your kid. They'll see the glow and think it's the coolest thing ever. Suddenly, your kid is a "Water Jedi," and will be occupied with the necessary task of defending the galaxy, so you can get them clean. You might need the lights back on to clean properly, of course.

HACK #3:

WHEN PAINTING THE HOUSE OR OTHER SURFACES, GIVE A BOARD TO YOUR KIDS TO PAINT, TOO.

Kids naturally want to be involved in the things you do. If you have a young child that wants to "help"—i.e., interfere with your house or fence painting—give them a small board of scrap wood to work on.

Lay down some newspaper and put the board on it. Give the child a small brush or sponge and a little paint and tell them they need to get this board painted. Make sure they're wearing paint-friendly old clothes, of course.

YOU'LL BE ABLE TO DISTRACT THEM FOR QUITE A WHILE, SO YOU CAN GET ON WITH THE FENCE OR THE HOUSE.

HACK #4:

GIVE A SMALL CHILD SOME WATER TO "PAINT" THE HOUSE OR FENCE WITH WHEN YOU'RE DOING THE REAL THING.

Another great way to keep your "helper" distracted is to give them a bucket of water and a small brush and ask them to "paint" the fence or whatever area you're not working on. They'll keep busy, and you can keep an eye on them and still get your own work done, whether it's painting or something else.

HACK #5:

PIZZA BOXES ARE ALSO GREAT FOR KEEPING YOUR KID BUSY.

We all love pizza, and more often than not, we end up getting it delivered in those flat cardboard boxes. When opened, a pizza box is large and makes a perfect "canvas" for your little one to draw on with crayons, paint with finger paints, etc. Since the boxes are probably already a bit messy from having pizzas in them, clean them off and then let your kid exercise their imagination.

THE MESSIER
THE BOX GETS,
THE BETTER, AND
IT WILL KEEP
THEM FOCUSED
ON ONE SMALL
AREA INSTEAD OF
ON YOUR WALLS,
FLOORS, OR
FURNITURE.

HACK #6:

GIVE YOUR KID SOME WOOD TO WORK ON (WITH PLAY TOOLS) WHILE YOU'RE WORKING.

If you have some woodwork to do (cutting, nailing, sanding, etc.) and your child wants to help (because of course they do), hand them a small piece to do their own "work" on—under your supervision, of course. You probably don't want to give them a real hammer and nails, but if they have toy tool kits, they can get to "work" on the board you give them, freeing up your time to get done what you need to get done.

HACK #7:

LOVE PLAYING VIDEO GAMES?

GIVE YOUR KIDS UNCONNECTED CONTROLLERS TO LET THEM "PLAY ALONG."

If you're serious about gaming, you have all the good stuff. And you want your time alone to really focus on the game at hand. But sometimes, you need to look after your kids, too. A great way to keep young children nearby without letting them interfere with your gameplay is to keep a controller or two as spares—ones that aren't connected to the console. Hand them out to your children and let them think they're playing along. They can do whatever they like, and it won't affect your game at all.

HACK #8:

ASSIGN SORTING CHORES TO KEEP YOUNGER KIDS BUSY.

Contrary to what you might think, a lot of kids like being given tasks. One easy way to keep younger kids busy is by letting them sort things by color, like felt balls, and put them into containers, like muffin tins or other small holders. The point here is not to actually give them something productive to do, but to keep them happy and occupied if you need a few minutes to attend to something else. They'll be proud of their work (and you should be too), and you'll get done what needs getting done.

CHAPTER 2

KEEPING IT CLEAN HACKS

HACK #9:

PUT PLASTIC WRAP OVER A GLASS AND PUNCTURE IT WITH A STRAW TO REDUCE SPILLS.

Spilled drinks are part of life for most kids, but it's a pain for parents, especially if it's in your brand-new car or on the living room carpet. An easy way to stop spills is to spread some plastic wrap over the top of the glass (be sure to have enough wrap securely down the sides) and then puncture a hole in the top with a straw. Your kids will have a fun way to drink, and you won't have to worry about having a big mess to clean up; at the very least, you'll have time to catch it before it splatters everywhere.

HACK #10:

KEEP RUBBER AND PLASTIC TOYS CLEAN AND FREE OF GERMS BY PUTTING THEM IN THE DISHWASHER.

Simple toys, especially for young children, can get gross and dirty pretty quickly. While you can hand-wash them, it's time-consuming and, let's face it, a bit gross. Check to see if they are dishwasher safe, of course, but a good trip through the washer will not only get them clean, it will disinfect them. Obviously, only toys that are washable can go in there, so don't try putting in anything that needs batteries.

HACK #11:

USE EMPTY CARDBOARD TOILET PAPER ROLLS AS EASY STORAGE FOR SMALL CARS AND OTHER TOYS.

Kids love their cars, and sometimes dads want to be right there with them, racing and zooming.

But if your kid has quite the collection, it can get a bit messy trying to keep them organized. An easy way to do this is to save cardboard TP rolls and stack them securely on a shelf (you can tape them together if needed).

EACH ROLL IS A SLOT FOR ONE CAR, LIKE A MINI GARAGE.

This is also good for small action figures; each one gets their own "bed" at the end of the day's adventure.

HACK #12:

USE CELLOPHANE TAPE TO CATCH NAIL CLIPPINGS.

Keep a bit of cellophane tape with you to collect cut nails as you trim them off, so that you don't have to go searching for nail bits everywhere afterward. This is especially true if you're clipping your kid's nails while they're asleep; you don't want loads of clippings to end up in the crib or the bed. Try to cut them into the tape and you can easily throw it away when you're done.

HACK #13:

USE WD-40 TO REMOVE CRAYON MARKS.

As you probably know, WD-40 has a lot of uses. And one of them could be very helpful if you have a little one who likes to draw on walls or other areas where they really shouldn't be drawing.

If your budding Leonardo da Vinci has left a masterpiece where there shouldn't be one, spray some WD-40 on a cloth and wipe over the crayon marks. They should come off easily. Be sure to gently wash away any leftover residue.

DEPENDING ON THE SURFACE, YOU CAN ALSO TRY USING TOOTHPASTE AND A LIGHT BRUSH.

HACK #14:

TOOTHPASTE CAN CLEAN PERMANENT MARKER SPOTS ON WOODEN FURNITURE.

Speaking of toothpaste, it works pretty well on permanent marker, too. If your kids have graduated from crayons to something a little more long-lasting, you can use toothpaste (not the gel kind—think baking soda) to remove their work. Smear a little on the mark and then take a damp cloth and begin to rub the spot. Do this for a minute or two, until the toothpaste gets rubbed in. Then wet the cloth and rub some more. The ink should start to lift. You might need to do it a few times, but the ink should eventually lift out.

HACK #15:

KEEP YOUR WALLS CLEANER BY GIVING YOUR CHILD A BIG, EMPTY BOX TO WORK ON.

Young kids love to get their crayons out and start drawing on any surface, but walls seem especially appealing.

So, what can you do when your mini Michelangelo wants to indulge in some art? Well, we get boxes of all kinds these days—some larger than others. If you have larger boxes (big enough for a kid to fit in), why not hand them over to your young artist?

THEY CAN SIT INSIDE AND BE SURROUNDED BY CANVASES.

They can go to town decorating the walls of the box however they like, keeping your actual walls safe.

HACK #16:

HAVE A SHOE RACK BY THE DOOR, SO KIDS' SHOES STAY IN ONE PLACE.

This is good practice for anyone, whether they have kids or not. Shoes pick up all kinds of gross stuff on a typical day out, as well as bacteria and viruses. So keeping shoes at the front door in a dedicated place is great for preventing germs and other unwanted things from getting tracked into the house.

AND YES, DAD, THAT MEANS YOU, TOO.

It sets a good example and gets your kids in the habit of a healthy practice that they'll take with them when they grow up. Leaving shoes at the door is common in many cultures around the world, so why not make it a part of your household too?

HACK #17:

USE A SHOE STORAGE BAG TO HOLD LEGOS AND OTHER BRICK TOYS.

Plastic shoe storage bags—the kind that hang on the backs of doors—are also ideal for storing Legos and other toys with multiple parts.

HANG THE BAG UP ON THE CLOSET DOOR IN YOUR CHILD'S BEDROOM, FACING OUTWARD.

You can separate out bricks by type and shape, so that each shoe slot is dedicated to one or a few kinds of bricks. This will not only keep things cleaner (and prevent the agony of stepping on a stray brick in the dark with your bare foot), but will also teach kids organizational skills and instill a commitment to keeping things clean and tidy.

HACK #18:

CLEAN LEGO BRICKS EASILY BY PUTTING THEM IN YOUR WASHING MACHINE.

No, this doesn't mean you should just chuck a bunch of them in there! That would end badly (probably in a washing machine repair). Get a laundry bag (the mesh zip-up kind) and put an article of clothing in it as padding. Then place some Lego bricks inside—not a huge amount, but you can probably put a decent number in there. Run it through the wash, remove the Legos from the bag, and let them dry naturally, which shouldn't take long. You'll want to avoid putting them in the dryer (noise plus dryer damage, plus the potential for melted plastic—yuck).

HACK #19:

MAKE CHORES INTO A GAME (SWEEPING INTO A SQUARE ON THE FLOOR, FOR EXAMPLE).

It's a good idea to instill some responsibility and work ethic in kids at a young age, and doing household chores is a great way to start. Of course, the idea of work and chores is going to bore them, and they'll protest; so why not make it into a game? This is especially good for younger children.

One example: put some masking tape on the floor in the shape of a square and assign your kid the task of sweeping everything into that square, after which it can be picked up. Like coloring, they have to stay inside the lines.

LITTLE CHALLENGES LIKE THIS MIGHT MAKE CHORE TIME MORE FUN.

HACK #20:

MISSING SOME THINGS?

Send your kids on a scavenger hunt to find them. Kids love organized hunts. Think of it like hide and seek. So if the remote, your keys, or something else has gone missing, make a game out of it and reward your child with a little something if they can find the missing item(s)—say, a treat or a snack. If you have more than one child, you can make it a competition (though be careful about rewarding one and not the other). A race against time is also fun.

HACK #21:

HAVE YOUR KIDS PICK UP THEIR TOYS WITH GRABBERS OR TONGS, WHICH MAKES THE PROCESS ITSELF A GAME.

Clean-up time is never fun, and if your kids have toys strewn all over the floor, it can be a real chore to get everything picked up and put away. So make a game out of it by buying some plastic grabbers, or using tongs you may already have in the house. Tell them they're going "excavating" to discover their toys, and that they have to pick up one at a time with the grabbers. Come up with silly rules and have fun; the cleaning up will be a lot less of a struggle, and they will enjoy it.

HACK #22:

LINT ROLLERS PICK UP GLITTER.

Kids love glitter. It's so...glittery. It's also a royal pain in the butt, and makes a mess that can never be undone, at least not completely. Seriously, you'll be finding it in drawers, under couch cushions, on your body, etc., long after they've gone away to college. Just embrace this and accept it. But that doesn't mean you need to go through life sparkling like a vampire from a YA novel.

A handy, simple lint roller will do wonders for picking up glitter spills and residue; just tear off sheets as they get glittered.

YOU WON'T BE ABLE TO PICK IT ALL UP, BUT YOU'LL SEE THE TABLE (OR FLOOR, OR COUCH) AGAIN.

HACK #23:

PUT A TARGET IN THE TOILET WHEN TRAINING A BOY TO PEE STANDING UP.

If you're trying to teach your young son to pee standing up, you're probably going have a few misses along the way, which means you'll be cleaning up more than you'd like to. A fun way to help train your young shooter is to put a waterproof sticker of a bullseye or a similar image in the toilet, maybe just above the drain. Tell your son he needs to try to hit the target every time. Offer a little reward if he hits it, say, five times in a row.

HACK #24:

KEEP YOUR TOILET PAPER FROM HANGING DOWN THE WALL.

Kids tend to pull off more toilet paper than they need, and they let the rest hang down, often all the way to the floor. If you have a cat, this is just an invitation to make an even bigger mess.

Don't waste toilet paper: put a fun sign on the wall underneath the roll stating that the paper is not allowed to hang below it. It can be in the design of a stop sign or a warning sign: "Halt! Go no farther!"

IT'S SILLY, BUT WILL REMIND THEM TO BE MORE AWARE OF THE RESOURCES THEY USE.

HACK #25:

USE HOT GLUE TO SHUT THE HOLES ON THE BOTTOM OF BATH TOYS; IT WILL STOP MOLD FROM GROWING IN THEM.

Most rubber bath toys have small holes somewhere—usually on the bottom. The problem is that if water gets into them (and it will), it's very difficult to get rid of it. And when that happens, mold can start to grow, and moldy smells can invade your bathroom. A simple solution is to take your trusty glue gun and glue these holes shut.

NO WATER CAN GET IN, SO NO MOLD CAN GROW.

HACK #26:

PUT COMMAND HOOKS ON THE BACK OF YOUR CHILD'S HIGHCHAIR AND HANG BIBS ON THEM.

Babies never run out of a need for bibs; as you probably know, feeding times get down-right messy. They're constantly being soiled, changed out, and washed, so a great way to always have a few on hand is to stick plastic hooks on the back of the highchair and use them to store all your bibs. That way they're within easy reach, and if a disaster happens (and you know it will), you can just reach around and get another bib.

HACK #27:

USE A PLASTIC GARBAGE BAG WITH A HOLE CUT IN IT WHEN GIVING YOUR KID A HOME HAIRCUT.

DIY haircuts are becoming increasingly popular, especially as the pandemic has kept people isolated and at home.

If you have the trimmers, but worry about the mess, a simple solution is to take a small trash bin liner and cut a circular hole in the middle. Place this over your kid's head and it will act like a barber's bib, keeping the hair off them.

DO THE TRIM OUTSIDE, AND YOU'LL HAVE AN EVEN EASIER TIME CLEANING UP.

HACK #28:

UNTANGLE DOLL HAIR WITH DISH SOAP AND HAIR CONDITIONER.

Dolls often have long hair, which can get pretty tangled through play and general use, just like human hair. If your child's dolls' hair is getting ratty and messy, you don't need to cut it off or wrangle it into plaits. You can usually just soak it in warm water with a bit of gentle dish soap (bonus: gets it clean), and then work some conditioner through it. This will detangle the hair for combing, and when it dries it will be good as new.

HACK #29:

SPRINKLE SOME BAKING SODA OR COFFEE GROUNDS ON FRESH PUKE.

It will absorb it and control the smell. In every life, a little puke must fall. Okay, if you're a parent, a lot of it.

YEAH, IT'S GROSS, AND YEAH, YOU HAVE TO DEAL WITH IT.

But there are ways to make it a little more bearable. Enter baking soda and/or coffee grounds. Both will start to absorb the mess (making it easier to clean up) and help diminish that nauseating aroma. Keep one or the other—or both—on hand at all times, since you never know when the next barf will blow.

HACK #30:

WEAR A BATHROBE OVER YOUR WORK CLOTHES IN THE MORNING.

So, you're all dressed for work, but you're feeding your baby, or getting the kids ready for school, and then something happens: the baby barfs, your kid launches some cereal in the air with a spoon, and suddenly you have a splatter all over your nice clean shirt or pants. The simple solution? Wear your bathrobe over your clean clothes. Let it be the armor that protects you from child-related mishaps so that you can take care of them and get on with your day. If your bathrobe meets with a mishap, you can just toss it in the wash and deal with it later.

CHAPTER 3

OUT & ABOUT HACKS

HACK #31:

SHOE ORGANIZERS ARE GREAT FOR ORGANIZING YOUR KID'S THINGS IN THE BACK SEAT OF YOUR CAR.

In addition to storage for Legos, a shoe orga-
nizer can be great to keep your kid's things
tidy and organized when you're on road trips.
Attach them to the front seats so that they hang
facing the kids sitting behind you.

Each compartment can be used for different things: toys, games, even small books, putting them all within easy reach without you having to fumble around while driving or pull over to get something.

BE CAREFUL ABOUT STORING FOOD IN THESE, THOUGH; THAT COULD BECOME MESSY.

HACK #32:

PLASTIC SHOWER CADDIES ARE GREAT FOR KEEPING THINGS CLEAN IN YOUR CAR WHILE YOU'RE EATING ON THE GO.

If you're on a road trip, you might have to eat while driving. And with kids in the back seat, that's almost a guaranteed messy disaster. One way to cut down on spills and various food items flying all over the place is to give each child a small plastic shower caddy, with each compartment filled with their food and drink (sandwiches, juice boxes, soda cans, chips, cookies, etc.), along with instructions to keep those things inside it. This will keep the food better organized and more likely to stay in the caddy, rather than end up all over the floor.

HACK #33:

USE A CAMERA BAG AS A DIAPER BAG—IT'S USEFUL WITH ALL THE COMPARTMENTS.

Camera bags have a ton of pockets and pouches, since photographers need everything but the kitchen sink on a shoot. But they also make great diaper/baby bags, too. With all those compartments, you have loads of places to store everything you need for a day out with your baby. And the design of the bag will make it easy to carry, since they're made for the long haul. Get a camera bag and use it only for this purpose; if you're into photography, you're going to want a separate bag, anyway.

HACK #34:

BRING AN EXTRA SHIRT FOR YOURSELF IN THE DIAPER BAG, JUST IN CASE.

This should be fairly self-explanatory. Accidents happen. Your baby will barf. It will get all over you. So be ready with a change of clothes, or at least a new shirt. And keep a plastic bag big enough to hold the soiled clothes, so you can wrap them up and keep them away from everything else.

BE PREPARED.

BARF IS INEVITABLE.

HACK #35:

WHEN YOU'RE ON A FAMILY OUTING, WRITE YOUR PHONE NUMBER ON YOUR KID'S ARM.

We never like to think about it, but sometimes kids get separated from us in crowds. If this happens, it can be a stressful—even panicky—situation. One way to help prevent something bad from happening is to mark your phone number in permanent marker (or use numbers from a temporary tattoo kit) on your child's arm, and tell your kid that if they get lost, they should go to a trusted adult (police officer, park ranger, etc.) and show them the number. The number won't wash or rub off and should be visible to anyone who sees it.

HACK #36:

DRESS YOUR KIDS IN THE SAME COLOR FOR OUTINGS.

Family outings are a must, and fun for everyone. In theory. But in big crowds, it can be a challenge to keep everyone together. If you have two or more kids, consider dressing them all in shirts of the same color so that they're easier to spot and it's easier for them to find each other. Losing a child in a crowd can be an awful experience for both parent and child, so make it a little easier to stay connected by identifying them with a distinct color before you head out: purple, red, etc.

HACK #37:

MAKE A "DAD CAVE" TO HELP YOUR CHILD SLEEP MORE EASILY.

When traveling with a baby or young child, one way to help them fall asleep more easily is to create a mini "cave" for them. All you need to do is hold them and place a soft cloth or blanket over them, covering their heads. It will block out light and even a bit of sound, and with luck, create a feeling of safety and peace, which just might help them go to sleep.

HACK #38:

HAVE DEDICATED ZIPLOCK BAGS FOR EACH KID'S OUTFITS IN THE SUITCASE.

When going on a trip, kids' clothes can get separated and lost—somehow more easily than adults' clothes. One way to keep everything together is to place a whole outfit (socks, underwear, pants, shirts, dresses, etc.) into a single large Ziplock bag, so that each bag has one complete set of clothes.

ROLL UP THE GARMENTS AND PLACE THEM INSIDE, THEN SET IN THE SUITCASE.

That way, you can also plan how many changes of clothes they'll need for the trip, and when you get to your destination, everything will be organized, so you can get on with enjoying your vacation.

HACK #39:

USE AN UPSIDE-DOWN CUP LID TO KEEP ICE CREAM FROM DRIPPING ALL OVER.

If you're out and it's a hot day, chances are your kids will want ice cream at some point, and you probably will too.

An easy way to keep ice cream from dripping all over everything is to put the wooden handle of an ice cream bar through the straw hole in an upside-down plastic lid. This will prevent ice cream from getting on their hands, and the edges of the upside-down lid will help prevent spilling and runoff.

AFTER THEY'RE DONE, YOU CAN THROW AWAY THE WHOLE THING.

HACK #40:

PUT CUPCAKE WRAPPERS IN YOUR CAR'S DRINK HOLDERS TO HELP PREVENT MESSES.

You might have a new car, SUV, or whatever. You're quite proud of it, but as a dad, you know that it will be used to transport your kids sooner or later, and you also know that this means your new car is going to get dirtied up really quickly. One spot that can get very messy and sticky right away is your car's drink holders. Even a little liquid dribbling down the side can collect at the bottom and make a gross mess. A simple solution? Put those little cupcake wrappers in the bottom of your drink holders. You can change them out with each trip. They'll catch the mess and keep your holders cleaner for longer.

HACK #41:

HAVE A SMALL PLASTIC CONTAINER FOR EACH PACIFIER WHEN TRAVELING TO KEEP THEM CLEAN.

Babies go through pacifiers quickly, and yes, they get gross quickly. One way to make sure that they stay clean for as long as possible is to store each one in a dedicated container. These could be Ziplock bags, salsa cups with lids, even leftover plastic containers from takeout (thoroughly washed, of course). Store as many as you need, each in a dedicated container, and you won't have to worry about them getting gross before they're used.

HACK #42:

This is kind of a silly hack, and it's mainly for your sanity on longer car drives.

IF YOU HAVE TWO OR MORE KIDS RIDING IN THE BACK SEAT OF YOUR CAR OR SUV, TRY FASTENING LARGE SHEETS OF CARDBOARD TO THE SEAT BETWEEN THEM.

This will create a compartment for each child to sit in, where they can't see each other. This might not work so well for older children, but for babies and toddlers, out of sight could well be out of mind. You'll be able to see all of them in your rear-view mirror, and it might make your trip a whole lot easier.

HACK #43:

TAKE PICTURES OF TOYS AT THE STORE, AND "EMAIL" THEM TO SANTA.

When you're out at the store, your children will probably point to things that they like and want—anything from candy to toys. Obviously, you can't indulge them every time they want something, so a great way to deflect is to pull out your phone, take a photo of the item, and tell your child that you'll be emailing the photo to Santa.

For young children who still believe, this is a fantastic way of changing the subject, and honestly, by the time the holidays roll around, they might have forgotten that they wanted it anyway.

SAVE THE PHOTOS AND YOU HAVE A GO-TO LIST FOR HOLIDAY SHOPPING.

HACK #44:

INSTEAD OF CARRYING THEM, HAVE YOUR TODDLER PRETEND TO PUSH YOU ALONG THE STREET.

Sometimes it's important to carry your toddler or small child; it might be for safety (crossing a road), they might be exhausted, etc. But sometimes, they'll just get used to being carried and want daddy to do it all the time. You're big and strong, right? Well, maybe you don't feel like it, and it's good to get them in the habit of moving themselves. So, if they want to be carried, make a game out of it. Tell them they have to "push" you up the street to the next block before you'll carry them. Allow your kids to gently shove you along; they'll probably love it, and you can reward them by carrying them for the next block. But be sure to put them down soon and make them push you again.

HACK #45:

KEEP BANDAGES EVERYWHERE.

This should come as no surprise, but kids and accidents are a match made in... heaven? Hell? You choose. They will most definitely get banged up, scraped, cut, and otherwise injured.

So be sure to keep a supply of assorted bandages with you at all times: in the car, in your laptop bag, in the stroller, in your phone case, etc.

YOU NEVER KNOW WHEN YOU'LL NEED ONE, AND YOU WILL NEED ONE.

HACK #46:

KEEP YOUR KIDS SAFE WHEN ON THE SIDES OF ROADS OR IN BUSY PARKING LOTS BY HAVING THEM TOUCH "THE SPOT."

Sometimes, you might need to pull over to the side of the road, or you might be in a busy shopping area, and you don't want your kids running out into traffic. A good way to keep younger children safe is to make a game of it: tell them that they have to touch "the spot." This could be the lid that covers the gas tank. You could tell them that they all have to keep their hands on the spot and not move until you say.

IT'S SIMPLE AND SLIGHTLY SILLY, BUT IT MIGHT SAVE A LIFE.

HACK #47:

MAKE AN "OUT OF ORDER" SIGN ON A PIECE OF PAPER AND KEEP IT IN YOUR WALLET.

Okay, this one is a bit sneaky and even unfair, but if you're in a hurry and you don't have time to stop, this can really help. Kids get distracted by all kinds of things, from vending machines to coin-operated animal rides. So if you see one in the distance that might cause a delay if someone suddenly wants to stop and linger, get ahead of them, whip out that sign, and hold it over the machine, ride, etc. You can tell them, "Sorry, the sign says it's not working," and be on your way. We told you it was sneaky and unfair, but sometimes you have to do what you have to do!

BRING CRAYONS TO THE DOCTOR'S OFFICE.

A visit to the doctor is scary for kids; heck, it's scary for adults. They won't like being in those rooms that seem so cold and clinical, and the presence of a tall stranger who wants to poke and prod them will just make things worse. For younger children, one way to calm them down while they wait is to bring some crayons and let them color on the disposable paper that's used on the examining tables and chairs. It will keep their minds off the scary doctor, at least until they show up, and might make them more at ease about the visit.

YOU MIGHT EVEN WANT TO TRY IT YOURSELF.

CHAPTER 4

SAFETY HACKS

HACK #49:

USE A BAKING SODA PASTE FOR SPLINTERS.

In every child's life, accidents will happen—some worse than others. While they might be minor, splinters can hurt like hell and be very difficult to remove. And going after them with sterilized needles and tweezers can just make things worse. Gently wash the skin. Add some baking soda to a dish. Add a small amount of water, just enough to make a thick paste. Put the paste over the splinter and secure with a bandage. Wait anywhere from an hour to twenty-four hours. The paste should have helped the splinter pop right out. Apply a little antibiotic ointment to the wound after the splinter is removed.

HACK #50:

STOP SLIPPERY SOCKS WITH GLUE.

No, you're not gluing your children to the floor—you're doing the next best thing. Socks tend to be slippery, and if you have hardwood or other non-carpeted floors, it's easy for kids to slip and fall if they're running around.

This can cause injuries, so it's a good idea to make those socks less slippery. Get a glue gun and write their names on the bottom of each pair of socks. Allow the glue to dry completely. The next time they wear them, no more slippage.

WASH THE SOCKS SEPARATELY IN COLD WATER AND LET THEM HANG DRY, BY THE WAY.

HACK #51:

USE A RULER TO BABY-PROOF A COLUMN OF DRAWERS.

If you have a tool chest or other storage cabinet with pull handles on the front of each drawer, and you want to keep toddlers or young children out (for safety reasons or whatever else), you can slide a ruler, yardstick, or other slender stick from the top down through each handle. This will prevent little hands from being able to open any of the drawers. Obviously, this only works with certain kinds of handles.

HACK #52:

USE BANDAGES TO BABY- AND KID-PROOF AN ELECTRICAL OUTLET.

Electrical outlets are generally safe, but if one of your kids gets the bright idea to stick something into the socket, it could be a very bad scene. Granted, this is more likely with babies and toddlers, but if you want to be sure that kids of any age are kept safe, one way to do it is to stick bandages over the outlets so that nothing can get into them. Of course, this is a temporary solution, but it will be enough to keep the baby safe, and should peel off just fine later on when you actually need the outlet.

HACK #53:

A FITTED SHEET MAKES AN EASY COVER FOR AN OUTDOOR CRIB.

If it's a nice day and you'd like your baby to be outside for a while, but are worried about bugs and sun, get a fitted sheet and stretch it over the top of the outside crib.

These kinds of cribs are usually mesh on the side to prevent insects from getting in, and you'll seal off the top with the sheet, making it virtually impossible for bugs to bother your baby. Place it under a tree for shade, and place your baby and appropriate toys inside before covering. You can sit outside and drink your iced tea (or other beverage of choice), all while keeping an eye on your baby.

EVERYBODY WINS.

HACK #54:

CUT YOUR CHILD'S NAILS AFTER THEY FALL ASLEEP.

This is usually more of a problem for babies and toddlers who don't want you fiddling with their fingers and toes, but it's necessary to cut their nails so that they don't get too long; if they do, your baby could end up scratching you both. It's usually a good idea to wait until about twenty minutes into their sleep cycle, when they're out cold. Then you can get to work, and they'll never even notice. Sneaky, but effective.

HACK #55:

AN INVERTED FITTED SHEET MAKES A GOOD OUTDOOR PLAYPEN.

Fitted sheets are a pain to fold (seriously, who knows how to do that?!), but for a baby or a toddler, they can make a great improvised playpen, like when you're out at the beach. You simply turn the sheet so that the downside is facing up, and then place four heavy-ish items on top of it, one in each corner (cooler, backpack, etc.). You'll have a simple little walled playpen to set your infant in that's easy to take down when you're done.

HACK #56:

A DRY INFLATABLE POOL IS A GREAT AND SAFE PLACE TO PUT YOUR BABY OUTDOORS.

If it's warm out and you want to enjoy the weather a bit, have some work to do, or there's a barbecue to get on with, using a small inflatable pool is a great way to provide a safe place for your baby while you do your work. You can keep them in your sight, fill the pool with toys, stuffed animals, and activities, and know that the soft and squishy walls will keep them from crawling away and getting into trouble.

HACK #57:

USE HONEY TO TREAT MINOR BURNS.

Childhood injuries are guaranteed, and if your little ones like messing around in the kitchen, there's a decent chance that they will get burned at some point. It's very important if this happens to inspect the burn right away and seek immediate medical attention if it appears serious.

But if it's a minor burn, like a quick singe from a hot tray, immerse the area in cool water (not ice cold) first for up to twenty minutes. Then spread a small amount of honey over the burn and cover lightly with a non-stick bandage.

HONEY'S NATURAL ANTIBACTERIAL PROPERTIES WILL HELP SOOTHE AND HEAL THE BOO-BOO.

HACK #58:

HONEY CAN SOOTHE A SORE THROAT.

If your child is ailing and has a sore throat, a sweet treat can sometimes soothe it. While some have said that marshmallows work well, there isn't any scientific evidence to support that. Honey, on the other hand, is soothing and has antibacterial and antiviral properties. A spoonful might make your sick child feel a little bit better, but of course, always consult a medical professional before trying any home remedies. Health blogs and parent websites can tell you what worked for them, but these are not a substitute for qualified medical advice.

HACK #59:

A POOL NOODLE UNDER A FITTED SHEET WILL KEEP YOUR KID FROM FALLING OUT OF BED.

We all did it when we were young: rolled out of bed and crashed unceremoniously to the floor. Getting used to sleeping in a bed without any railings is a major transition from toddlerhood to childhood. While you could spend money on a guard rail to slide under the mattress, a simple and inexpensive barrier to prevent your kid from ending up on the floor is the humble pool noodle. Simply slide one under the fitted sheet and move it to the edge of the bed (you can put one on each side). It will be tall enough to prevent your young one from tumbling out of bed, and easy to take out during the day.

HACK #60:

PUT THE MATTRESS ON THE FLOOR.

THIS IS ONLY A TEMPORARY SOLUTION.

If the pool noodle isn't working, another option is to simply take your child's mattress and put in on the floor for a while. It might help them get used to sleeping in a bed without rails, and if they do happen to roll off, it's a very short drop to the floor. After they get comfortable with this new arrangement, you can put the bed back on the frame and see how it goes.

HACK #61:

PRACTICE SELF-DEFENSE.

Okay, it's going to happen. At some point, your kid is going to accidently whack you: in the face, in the stomach, or worst of all, between the legs. Injuries in the name of fatherhood come with the territory, so it's good to be ready in case your kids get a little out of hand.

Keep your hands at the ready when lying in bed, should your kid try to jump on your chest. A hand in the pocket can act as a first line of defense against a nut attack. Tilting your head to one side or another when your kid is sitting in your lap might prevent their head from smashing your nose head-on.

BE SENSIBLE. LOOK FOR DANGER ZONES AND REACT ACCORDINGLY.

HACK #62:

USE A SLICE OF BREAD TO CLEAN UP BROKEN GLASS.

In every parent's life, they will likely encounter some broken glass. And to make sure it doesn't get stuck in little hands or feet, you need to be on it right away. A simple method for cleaning up glass shards on the floor or table is to use a piece of sliced bread. Simply take the slice and press it down over the area where the glass shards are.

THEY WILL STICK TO THE BREAD WHEN YOU LIFT IT UP AND YOU CAN TOSS IT OUT SAFELY.

Shine a flashlight over the whole area to make sure you've picked up every piece; glass has a tendency to fly out in multiple directions, so look beyond where you think it all is, just to be sure.

HACK #63:

BUILD A CHILD-PROOF FENCE AROUND YOUR GRILL.

You love grilling in the summertime. And your family loves those barbecued burgers, hot dogs, kebabs, and more for outdoor dinners. But grills are dangerously hot, and little hands that get too close to them could get badly burned. For toddlers, your best bet is to build a little fence around the grill, one you can easily step over, but which will be impassable to your two-year old. Indoor child gates can be repurposed into a fence, and your local hardware store might have other materials and ideas.

HACK #64:

LOCK-PROOF YOUR BEDROOM AND BATHROOM DOORS WITH A RUBBER BAND.

If you have doors with locks that could potentially get your young kids stuck somewhere (a bedroom or bathroom, for example), take a rubber band and place it over the door handle on one side. Stretch it toward the outside of the door and twist it in an "x" shape over the shutting mechanism, then loop it over the door handle on the other side. The door will still be able to shut, but the mechanism will be held in place and won't be able to slide into the door frame, potentially locking someone in or out.

HACK #65:

USE FROZEN MARSHMALLOWS AS AN ICE PACK.

If your kid gets a mild sprain or bump (and you know it will happen) and you want to put something cold on it, an adult ice pack can sometimes be too intense for them. Instead, keep some marshmallows in a plastic storage bag frozen in the freezer. They will be cool but not freezing, and can be a great way to get something cold on a sprain without it making your accident-prone little one even more uncomfortable.

CHAPTER 5

SNACK HACKS

HACK #66:

FREEZE BABY FOOD IN AN ICE TRAY TO HAVE A WEEK OR MORE OF SERVINGS READY.

Ice cube trays are great for many things other than ice. One idea that works well is to fill each cube space with a portion of baby food and then freeze it, so that you have ready-made portions that can be thawed (or briefly micro-waved) and served. You can have a week or more of servings at hand this way—and have different flavors ready to go—or have a different tray for each type of food.

HACK #67:

USE A PIZZA CUTTER TO CUT PANCAKES INTO SMALL SQUARES FOR TODDLERS AND YOUNG CHILDREN.

Pancakes and waffles are awesome, but even dads with big mouths still need to use a knife and fork to cut them down to size.

If you have toddlers that want to partake in the glory of the pancake, one way to make it easier to eat is to use a pizza cutter (the wheeled kind) to cut said pancake into little squares, or even pizza slices, so that your toddler has bite-sized pieces at the ready.

MAKE A BIG DEAL OUT OF CUTTING THEM IN FRONT OF YOUR CHILD, SO THAT IT'S FUN AND A SPECIAL TREAT.

HACK #68:

TOO MUCH HALLOWEEN CANDY?

NO PROBLEM!

Halloween is awesome, but maybe your kids have come back with a little more candy than they should probably eat.

Of course, they'll want to tear into it, but you can give them an alternative: offer them a prize for a certain number of pieces of candy, such as movie tickets, an extra hour of video gaming, etc. It doesn't have to be a big prize, but it needs to be something they'll value, so that they're willing to part with some of their loot. And what do you do with all that extra candy?

SECRETLY EAT IT YOURSELF, OF COURSE!

HACK #69:

HIDE CANDY BY PUTTING IT IN EMPTY BAGS OF FROZEN VEGETABLES, THEN STORE IN THE FREEZER.

If your kids are helping themselves a little bit too much to the candy on your shelves, you can hide some of it by putting it in an empty (i.e., used up) bag of frozen broccoli, asparagus, or whatever else makes them gag. Just put the candy in there, clip the top shut, and put it back in the freezer.

THE CANDY WILL KEEP LONGER, AND THEY'LL NEVER GO ANYWHERE NEAR IT.

HACK #70:

SLICE FRUITS AND VEGGIES INTO FRENCH FRY SHAPES.

Let's face it, kids love french fries, and as a dad, you do too. But sometimes, it really is better for your kids to eat something other than a big mess of greasy fries, yummy as they are. It's good for them to have fruit and vegetables (okay, technically the potato is a vegetable, but still).

So, what to do? Try slicing up some apples, celery, carrots, etc., into the same shape and size as french fries. No, it's not the same, but sometimes making healthy snacks into "kid-sized" shapes can make it more fun for them to eat them.

AND YOU CAN SECRETLY HAVE ALL THE REAL FRIES TO YOURSELF.

HACK #71:

IF YOUR KID HATES CERTAIN KINDS OF FOOD, HIDE THEM IN A SMOOTHIE.

Yes, this is another one of those sneaky hacks, but it's very effective. Things like veggies (carrots, spinach, and broccoli) can easily be cooked and blended in with bananas, strawberries, yogurt, etc. They'll be drinking a healthy beverage full of fruit, and the hated veggies will slip right on in unnoticed. Of course, certain greens will change the color of the smoothies, so you can add a little fresh mint and tell them it's a "dragon smoothie" or some such. Treachery and deceit are your friends. Use them often.

HACK #72:

CHANGE UP YOUR DINNER ROUTINES FROM TIME TO TIME.

For fun, try having dinner in places other than the dinner table. And no, not in front of the TV. Try sitting under the table. Put a picnic blanket down on the living room floor.

IF IT'S WARM, EAT OUT IN YOUR BACKYARD.

Make dinner fun and new once in a while, and you might just have some more enthusiastic eaters as a result!

HACK #73:

COOK A LOT OF HOT DOGS AT ONCE BY USING A CROCK-POT.

Your child is having a birthday party and has invited thirty-seven of their closest friends... hooray! Except you're the one that has to feed them. Now, you could go out to the grill and do the "manly" thing—trying to cook hot dogs and burgers a few at a time while very hungry children get irritated.

Or you can cook dozens of dogs in advance by using a simple Crock-Pot. Simply put them in the pot (seriously, like forty or more), don't add water (they have enough of their own), and cook on low for four hours.

THEY'LL BE READY AT THE SAME TIME, AND YOU CAN SERVE EVERY HUNGRY MOUTH AT ONCE.

HACK #74:

PROGRAM YOUR COFFEE MAKER AHEAD OF TIME.

Coffee is life, at least as far as weekday mornings go. You might not be able to function without it, which is going to make getting your kids ready for school even harder. The old joke is that people often need coffee to make coffee. So, do just that. Program your coffee maker the night before and make sure that you have a fresh pot ready for when you get up. Your kids will thank you, and you'll thank yourself.

CHAPTER 6

FUN AT HOME HACKS

HACK #75:

PUT A LAUNDRY BIN IN THE BATH AND SET YOUR CHILD IN IT; THEN THEIR TOYS WON'T FLOAT AWAY.

Young children need all kinds of distractions to make baths bearable (see Hack #2). But too many toys in the bath, and they'll all start to float away, out of reach. If the child is busy trying to get them back, it makes bathing harder (as if it wasn't hard enough). So, for small children, set a large plastic laundry bin in the tub first, and then fill with water as usual. Put your child and the toys in the bin and wash as normal.

THEN ALL THE TOYS WILL BE EASY TO GRAB.

HACK #76:

MAKE ACTIVITIES INTO A RACE TO GET THEM DONE.

It can be a struggle to have your kids get dressed, get ready for bed, pick up toys, and so on. Somehow, these normally energetic little beings become instantly sluggish when it comes to doing things they don't want to do.

LET'S BE HONEST— WE ALL DO THAT.

But one way to make them a little more efficient is to turn the unpleasant event into a race. It might be against each other (if you have two or more kids) or just a race against the clock. A small reward for the winner could even be in order (they get to stay up a few minutes past bedtime, or some such). They'll have fun racing and whatever needs doing will get done much quicker.

HACK #77:

MAKE A STAIR SLIDE OUT OF CARDBOARD PIECES.

Okay, this is totally a "dad" thing, but if you live in a home with stairs (straight, not spiraled), you can try this hack out—as safely as possible, of course. Get some thick, wide cardboard sheets, and lay them down on the stairs from top to bottom.

Now your kids, if small enough, should be able to sit on some cloth at the top of the stairs and ride down to the bottom.

IT'S AN INSTANT INDOOR SLIDE!

Just be sure you check with your spouse about this one first; they might be less than thrilled.

HACK #78:

USE PLASTIC STORAGE CONTAINERS TO MAKE SNOW BRICKS.

If you live in an area that gets enough snow in the winter, one great way to help your kids with their all-important snow construction work is to use a set of identical plastic storage containers, like Tupperware.

USE THESE TO SCOOP OUT SNOW INTO BRICK SHAPES.

These can then be easily stacked to form snow forts, makeshift igloos, or whatever they want. Of course, getting them to shovel the snow later is whole different thing.

HACK #79:

MASKING TAPE LAID OUT ON THE CARPET OR FLOOR MAKES A GREAT RACETRACK FOR YOUR CHILD'S TOY CARS.

Toy cars are at their best when they have a place to race around, right? And of course, having a dedicated track for them is even better. But sometimes, it's just not feasible to set up a big, complicated thing. A simple, temporary solution is to lay down some strips of masking tape on the floor to create makeshift racetracks; have them help with the design. You can make a fun place to race their cars and it's easy to clean up afterward, with no damage to the floor.

HACK #80:

FILL A CAMPING TENT WITH SAND FOR A DAY AT THE BEACH IN YOUR BACKYARD.

A day at the beach is not always an option, and having a dedicated sandbox might not work, either. One way around that, if your children want to play in some sand, is to have a camping tent on hand and fill it with a layer of sand so they can play in it. The bonus is that if it's really hot and sunny, they'll be protected inside the tent, while still having the fun of puttering around in the sand. You can dispose of the sand later when they've finished, and refill as needed.

HACK #81:

DINING ROOM TABLES CAN MAKE GREAT PILLOW FORTS.

Really, this should be fairly obvious. When not in use for dining, drape a sheet over the top of the table and stuff the sides with pillows, cardboard boxes, stuffed animals, and whatever else comes to mind.

YOU HAVE AN INSTANT FORT WITH A SUPER ROOF ON IT.

It works so well, you might want to just do it up for yourself and shoo the kids away.

HACK #82:

IN WARM WEATHER, USE AN ELECTRIC FAN TO POOF UP A PILLOW (OR OTHER) FORT.

Sheets draped over pillows or tables can make a great private fort, but they can also get droopy.

A fun way to puff them up (especially in warm weather), is to place an electric fan inside and let it blow.

ALL OF A SUDDEN, THE SHEETS ARE BILLOWING OUT INSTEAD OF FALLING IN, AND THE FORT JUST GOT BIGGER.

HACK #83:

TO MAKE A FUN SOUND, PUT A ZIP TIE OR TWO AGAINST THE BACK WHEEL OF YOUR KID'S BICYCLE OR TRICYCLE.

This is a modern variation on that old kids' trick of putting a baseball card by the wheel to clatter against the spokes as they turned.

YOU HAVE TO WONDER: HOW MANY VALUABLE CARDS WERE DESTROYED?

How many Hank Aarons and Babe Ruths ended up in the trash? A zip tie is a better option, anyway; it will last longer and make a louder noise. Have at it, and let your kids experience the fun of clacking wheels.

HACK #84:

SET UP A KID-FRIENDLY PLAYLIST FOR MORNING MOTIVATION.

Are your kids sluggish about getting up for school?

OF COURSE THEY ARE.

So why not make a playlist of some of their favorite songs to play on your phone at breakfast to get them in a happier mood, and maybe motivate them to get going? It's no guarantee, but it might lighten the mood a bit, and make the before-school time a little more fun.

CHAPTER 7

MISCELLANEOUS DAD HACKS

HACK #85:

TEACH YOUR KIDS THE DIFFERENCE BETWEEN THE RIGHT AND LEFT SHOE WITH STICKERS.

Buy a sticker of something your kid likes (a cartoon character, a superhero, etc.). Cut it in half. Place the left half in the left shoe and the right half in the right shoe, so that when the shoes are next to each other, you can see the whole image. This will teach your kids which shoe goes on which foot, because they'll want to make sure the picture matches up before they put their feet in. You'll probably have to change these out pretty frequently, but with luck, it won't take long for your child to learn the difference, anyway.

HACK #86:

TEACH YOUR KIDS ABOUT MANAGING THEIR TIME WITH A COLORED-IN CLOCK.

One way to show kids how to manage their time is to take an inexpensive analogue clock (i.e., with all twelve numbers on it) and color in sections, like triangles on a pie chart.

You might make the 5 to 6 triangle green and have a chart underneath that explains that green indicates cleaning up and getting ready for dinner. 7 to 8 could be colored blue, with a corresponding note on the chart stating that this is the time for homework. You could have a clock for weekdays and a clock for weekends, or one for mornings and one for evenings.

THE BONUS IS THAT YOUR KIDS WILL LEARN HOW TO TELL TIME THE OLD-FASHIONED WAY.

HACK #87:

MONSTERS IN THE CLOSET KEEPING YOUR KIDS AWAKE?

Give them a monster-repellant spray gun. Most children are afraid of the dark—at least sometimes. They might think that there's something in the closet, under the bed, or by the window. Little imaginations can run wild in the dark, so help them out by giving them a means of defending themselves and confronting the monster directly. Get a plastic spray bottle and decorate it or write on it; make it personalized to your kid. Put a little water in it and set the nozzle to mist.

HAVE THEM PRACTICE WITH IT.

When the monster comes back, they can grab the bottle by their bed and shoot it with a little harmless mist. Monster is gone, and your kids learn a bit about standing up for themselves.

HACK #88:

STROKING A BABY'S FACE WITH A SOFT TISSUE CAN OFTEN GET IT TO SLEEP VERY QUICKLY.

Babies can get upset for all kinds of reasons, and often it seems like they just cry for the sake of crying. If your infant is having issues going to sleep, here's a simple thing you can try to calm them down: take a soft tissue and gently stroke your baby's face on the cheek and the forehead. The soft motion of the stroking is calming and soothing. Many parents have reported that it puts the baby to sleep in a hurry, so give it shot the next time you need some calm and quiet.

HACK #89:

TAKE AWAY CHARGERS TO TEACH A LESSON ABOUT CONSERVING ENERGY AND USING DEVICES WISELY.

SOMETIMES, KIDS NEED TO BE TAUGHT LESSONS.

This isn't about punishment, per se, but about teaching them to see a bigger picture. If your kid is always on their device, and you'd like to get them off it and back into the real world at dinner and other times, one idea you can try is to take away the charger. Then they will have a limited amount of time before their device shuts down and will be more careful about wasting time on it. You can give the charger back once every few days to teach them to use their time more wisely.

HACK #90:

HAVE THEM DO A CHORE IN EXCHANGE FOR THE WI-FI PASSWORD.

Yeah, your kids probably love the internet as much as you do and want to spend all their time on it. And that can be a problem, for a lot of reasons. It's good to limit their online time, just as you would for TV, video games, and other such electronic things. One way to make the internet more "valuable" for your kids is to offer the password (which you should change frequently) in exchange for a chore. Maybe they get one hour for each one job done, and then have to do another chore for another hour. Having them work a little for their time will make it more valuable, and probably less wasted.

HACK #91:

WARM A TOILET SEAT FOR THOSE COLD MORNINGS.

Note: this only works if you have a toilet seat that is not closed off in a full circle, but has both sides open with a gap in between, like those in most public restrooms. If you do have an open-ended seat, you can cut down on the shock of the freezing seat (and a lot of complaining from your kids) by putting some old (but clean) socks over each side, covering up the cold.

MAKE SURE THE SOCKS ARE LONG ENOUGH TO REACH UP BOTH SIDES.

Then your kids can sit in peace and comfort, and you can easily wash the socks later.

HACK #92:

YOU CAN UPCYCLE A BABY COT INTO A NEW TABLE FOR YOUR TODDLER.

Once your baby grows out of their crib, you have a nice piece of furniture that you no longer need. One great way to get more use out of it is to take off one long side of the railing.

PUT A SHEET OF WOOD OVER THE BEAMS AND YOU'LL HAVE A NICE TABLE FOR A SMALL CHILD TO SIT AT.

The high walls on the other three sides will ensure that nothing gets knocked off, and they'll have a little work desk perfectly suited to their size for coloring, painting, and whatever else they can dream up.

HACK #93:

USE A TISSUE TO HELP YOUR KID LEARN HOW TO HOLD A PENCIL.

When young children are learning to write, it can be a challenge to get them to hold the pencil correctly. One easy way to help with this new task is to take a small piece of tissue and have your child hold it by curling their pinky and ring fingers down to clutch it to their palm. Then the middle and index finger and thumb can grasp the pencil. It's an easy way to show them how to hold the pencil properly, like training wheels for a writing instrument.

HACK #94:

ATTACH YOUR REMOTES TO YOUR COFFEE TABLE SO THEY DON'T GO MISSING.

Your kids love the remotes almost as much as you do. And there's a good chance that if they're using one of them to watch afternoon cartoons or some such, it will eventually end up going missing. In fact, it's inevitable.

One way to fix this is to glue spiral rubber cords to each remote (like old telephone lines) and attach them securely to your coffee table or whatever else you have sitting by your couch.

THAT WAY, THE REMOTES WILL NEVER BE MISSING WHEN IT'S YOUR TURN TO USE THEM.

HACK #95:

BE FLEXIBLE ABOUT BEDTIME OCCASIONALLY.

This might seem counterintuitive at first, but if you think about it, it's not a bad idea. No kid likes going to bed on an enforced schedule, even though it's important to get them into a routine. So, while enforcing that routine, be willing to loosen it up once in a while.

IS YOUR KID ABSORBED IN A BOOK THAT THEY CAN'T PUT DOWN?

Give them an extra ten minutes to finish the chapter. Is the whole family having a great time with a game? Let it last a little longer. Minor changes like this are actually beneficial, if something good is coming out of them.

HACK #96:

USE A BABY BACKPACK WHILE WORKING ON OTHER THINGS.

Let's face it, you're busy. You need to be able to watch your baby, but you can't just sit with them all day. You have things to do. The solution? A baby backpack, of course. These wonderful inventions are worth the investment and will allow you to carry your infant with you and still be hands-free to get on with whatever you have to do. A great idea, unless you're putting your head under the hood of your car or something.

HACK #97:

TEACH YOUR KIDS COOPERATIVE GAMES FIRST AS AN INTRODUCTION TO COMPETITIVE GAMES AND HOW TO BE A GOOD LOSER.

Yes, we get it. You want your kid to be a sports star, or even just to succeed in a competitive world. But getting too heavy with the competitive vibes early on is often not a good idea. Kids need to socialize, and learning games that don't pit them against each other can teach them a lot about teamwork and contributing. There are many good resources for these kinds of games, and from there you can move them on to baseball, soccer, skating, or whatever.

LEARNING TO BE A PART OF A TEAM CAN HELP WHEN THEY— INEVITABLY— LOSE AT SOMETHING.

HACK #98:

PUT TAPE OVER THE SPEAKERS ON LOUD TOYS TO BRING DOWN THE VOLUME.

Let's face it, some battery-operated toys are just obnoxious. While they might be entertaining for your kids, they can really get on your nerves.

You know the ones: they play the same insipid song over and over, have some annoying voice, etc. One way to cut down on the irritation factor is simply to place a little cellophane tape over the speaker, wherever it might be. This will mute the sound without blocking it completely. Your child will still be able to hear it, but if they're in another room, you probably won't.

PEACE AT LAST!

HACK #99:

SPRINKLE CINNAMON IN THE SAND TO DISCOURAGE BUGS FROM GETTING IN YOUR CHILD'S SANDBOX.

Kids love playing in sandboxes; it's like having a little bit of the beach at home. Unfortunately, sand can attract ants, centipedes, flies, and other creepy-crawlies. So, if you're filling up your child's sandbox, add a cup of cinnamon to the sand and mix it in thoroughly.

IT SMELLS NICE AND KEEPS THE BUGS AWAY.

Ants especially hate cinnamon. Just make sure that the sand is not so appealing to your little one that they want to eat it.

HACK #100:

BE WILLING TO "OUTSOURCE" THE THINGS YOU DON'T DO WELL.

Let's face it, we're all only human. You might feel like Superdad one day and then crash and burn the next. That's normal, and it's okay. Being a parent is a constant learning experience, but you'll find over time that you're better at some things than others.

Talk with your spouse about this; they might be willing to take over some chore you hate, while you can offer to do something they're not good at. Or maybe it's time to bring in some help from the outside.

WHATEVER YOU DECIDE, JUST REMEMBER THAT YOU DON'T HAVE TO GO IT ALONE.

SO,
THERE YOU
HAVE IT.

One hundred dad hacks that might make your life a little easier, and your kids' lives a little more fun. Give these a try, change them up a little, make up new ones of your own... do whatever you like. You'll appreciate taking the time to try some of them out, and if you have a spouse or partner, they will too. Happy dadding!

ABOUT CIDER MILL PRESS BOOK PUBLISHERS

Good ideas ripen with time. From seed to harvest, Cider Mill Press strives to bring fine reading, information, and entertainment together between the covers of its creatively crafted books. Our Cider Mill bears fruit twice a year, publishing a new crop of titles each spring and fall.

CIDER MILL PRESS

BOOK PUBLISHERS

Visit us online at
cidermillpress.com

or write to us at
PO Box 454
12 Spring Street
Kennebunkport, Maine 04046